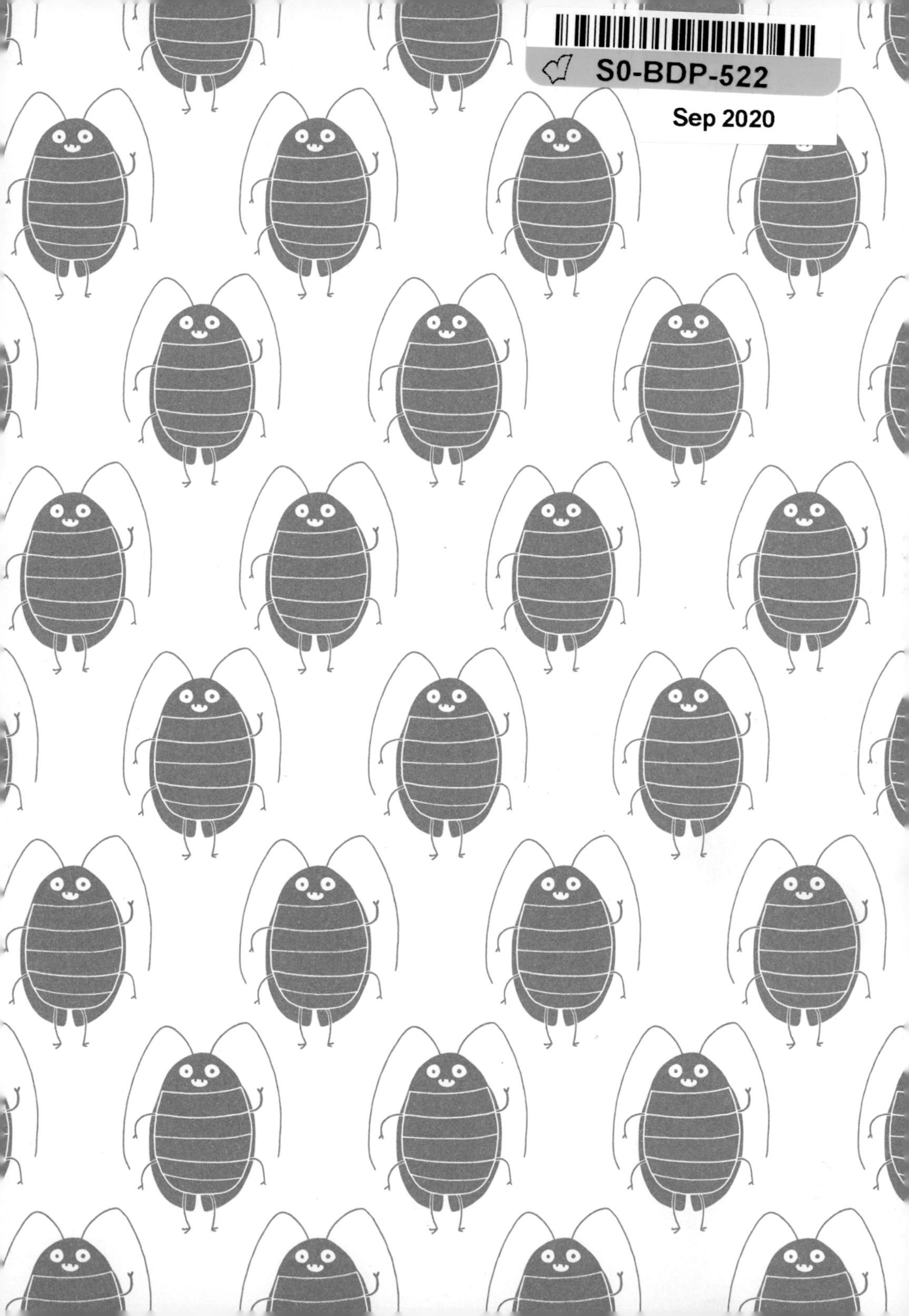

THE COCKROACH

Tundra Books, an imprint of Penguin Random House Canada Young Readers, a Penguin Random
House Company

Library and Archives Canada Cataloguing in Publication

Library and Archives Canada Cataloguing in Publication
Title: The cockroach / Elise Gravel.
Other titles: Coquerelle. English
Names: Gravel, Elise, author.
Series: Gravel, Elise. Petits dégoûtants. English.
Description: Series statement: Disgusting critters | Translation of: La coquerelle.
Identifiers: Canadiana (print) 20190141816 | Canadiana (ebook) 20190141832 | ISBN 9780735266421
(hardcover) | ISBN 9780735266438 (EPUB)
Classification: LCC QL505.5 .G7213 2020 | DDC j595.7/28—dc23

Published simultaneously in the United States of America by Tundra Books of Northern New York,
an imprint of Penguin Random House Canada Young Readers, a Penguin Random House Company

Library of Congress Control Number: 2019944412

English edition edited by Samantha Swenson
Designed by Elise Gravel and Tundra Books
The artwork in this book was rendered digitally.

Printed and bound in China

www.penguinrandomhouse.ca

1 2 3 4 5   24 23 22 21 20

Penguin Random House | TUNDRA BOOKS

Elise Gravel

THE COCKROACH

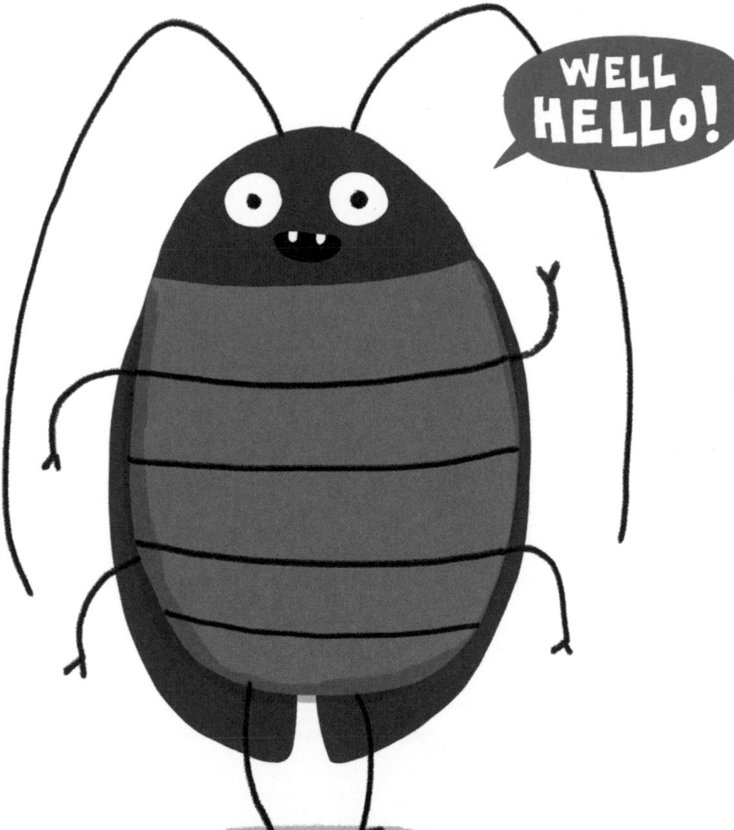
WELL HELLO!

tundra

My dear readers, allow me to introduce my friend

COCKROACH.

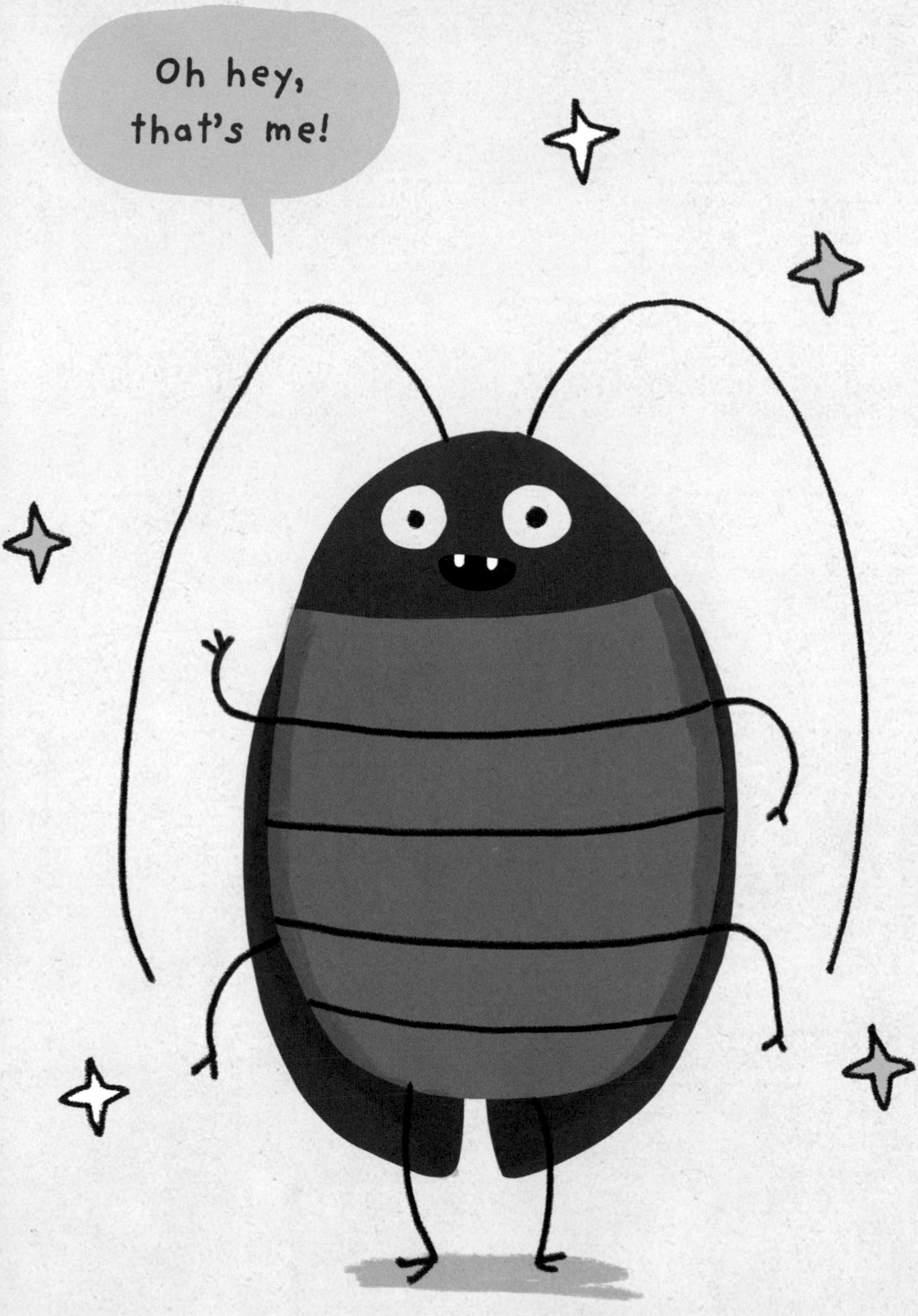
Oh hey, that's me!

In this book we will be talking about the American

COCKROACH,

but other species of cockroaches are known as

PALMETTO BUGS

OR

CROTON BUGS.

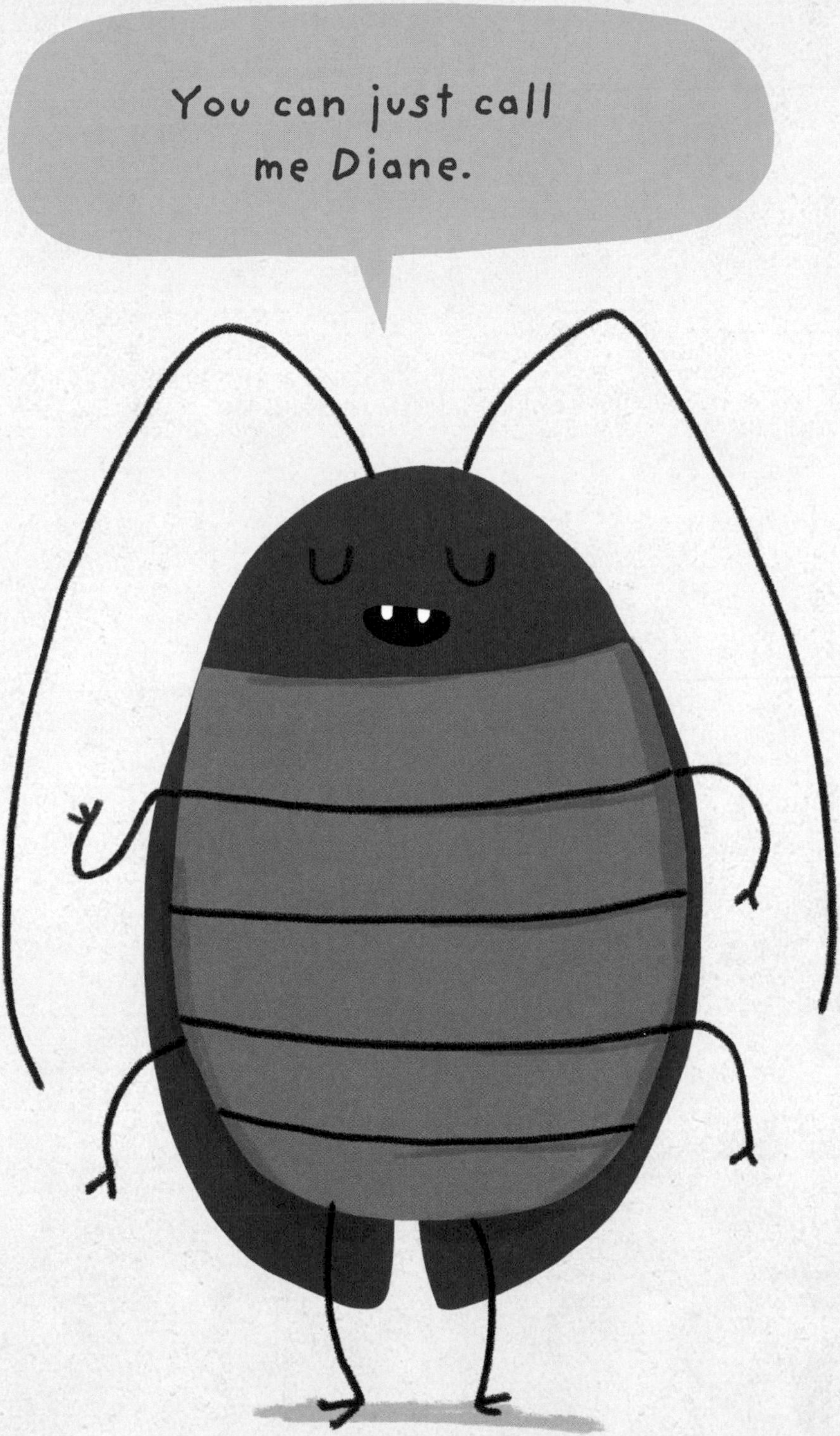
You can just call me Diane.

The cockroach measures about an inch and a half, or 4 centimeters, and is

OVAL

shaped and flat. She is reddish brown, but in other parts of the world, there are brightly colored and patterned species too.

I put on my leopard-print outfit in case I get on TV.

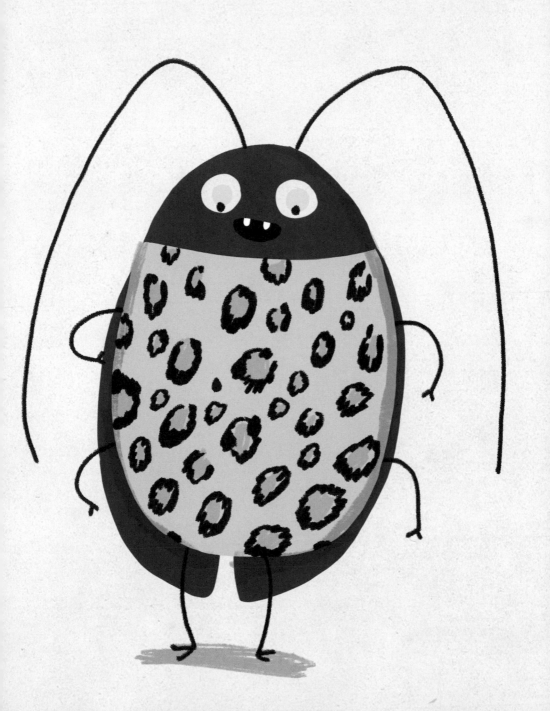

The cockroach has antennae that are almost as long as her body and little hairs on her abdomen that allow her to detect the slightest movement. She also has mandibles that act like teeth or a

Cute, huh?

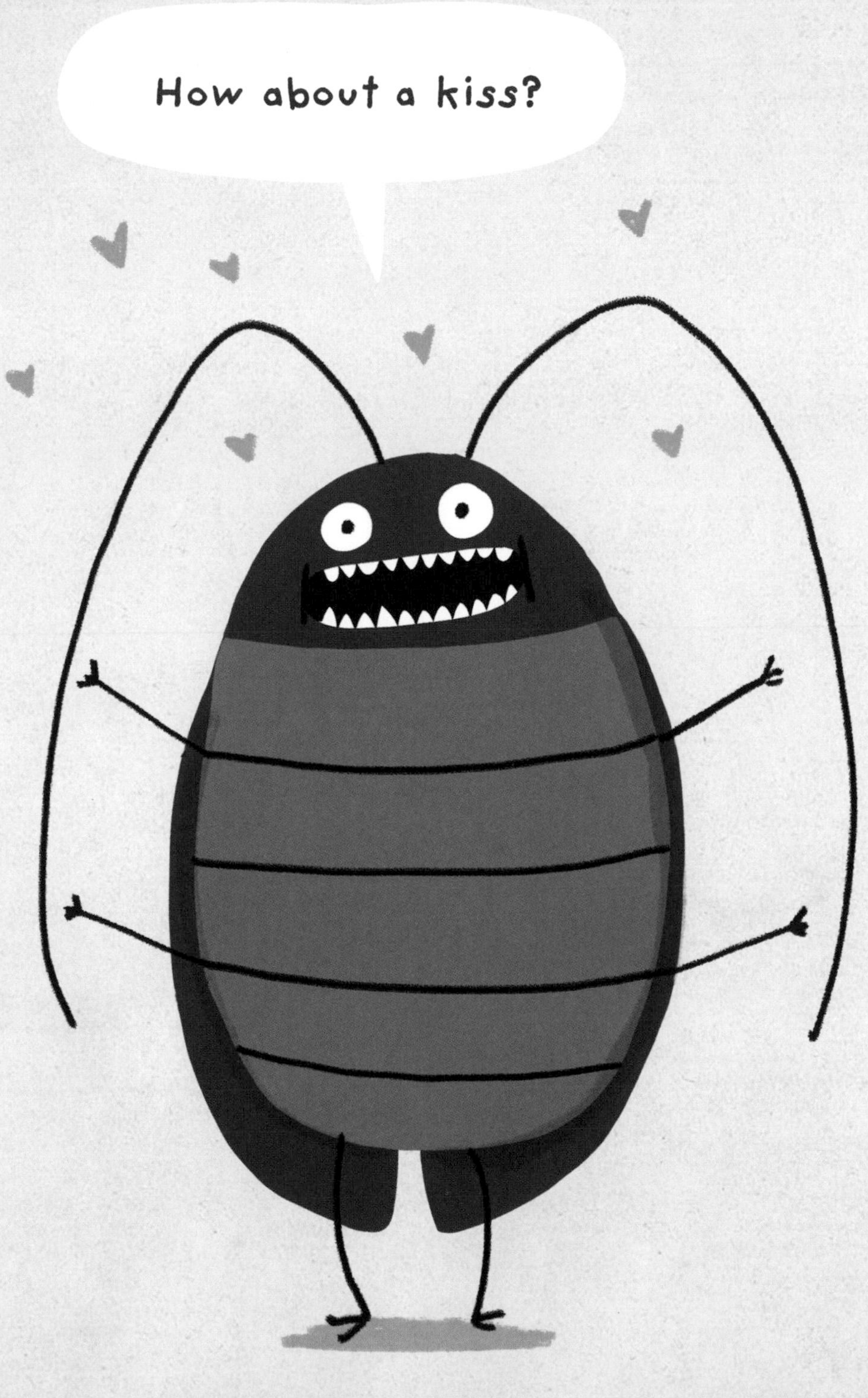
How about a kiss?

The cockroach has wings, but she almost never flies. She is, however, a pretty fast runner. She can move at speeds up to 3 miles, or 5 kilometers, an hour. This makes her among the

FASTEST

running insects in the world.

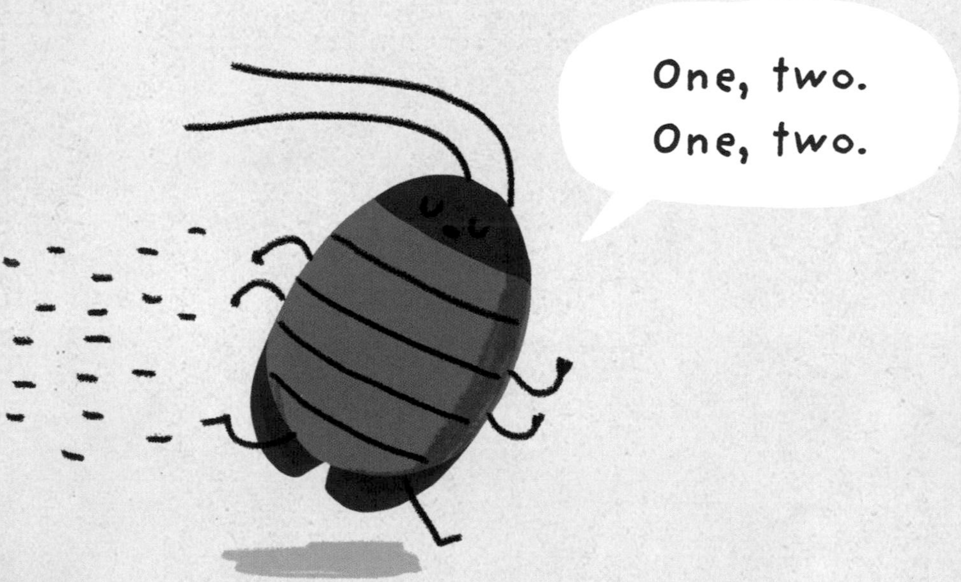
One, two.
One, two.

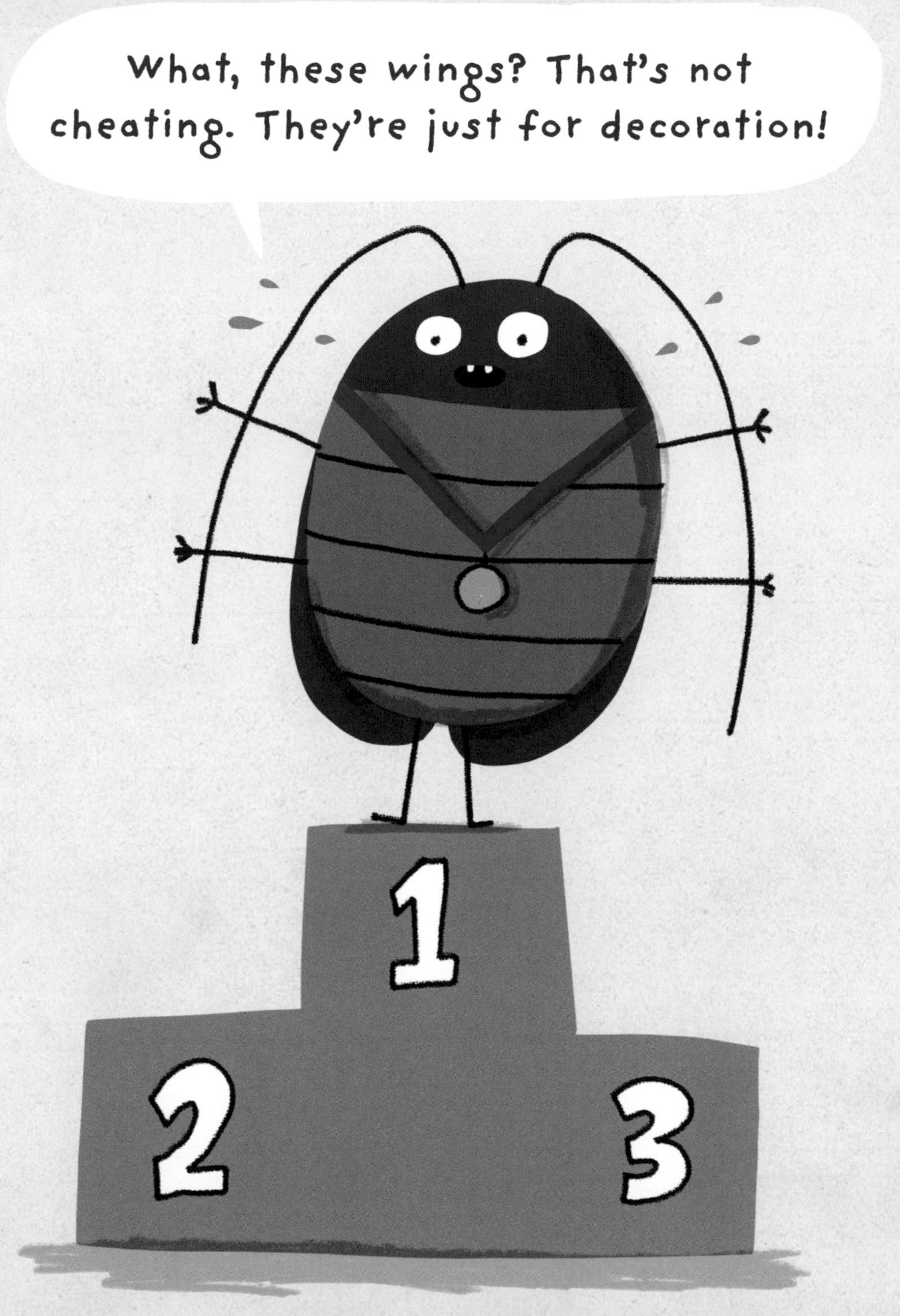
What, these wings? That's not cheating. They're just for decoration!
1
2
3

The cockroach hates

LiGHT.

She spends her days hidden away and prefers to come out at night. When a cockroach colony grows big enough, though, they will start coming out in daylight.

I wear sunglasses so no one will recognize me.

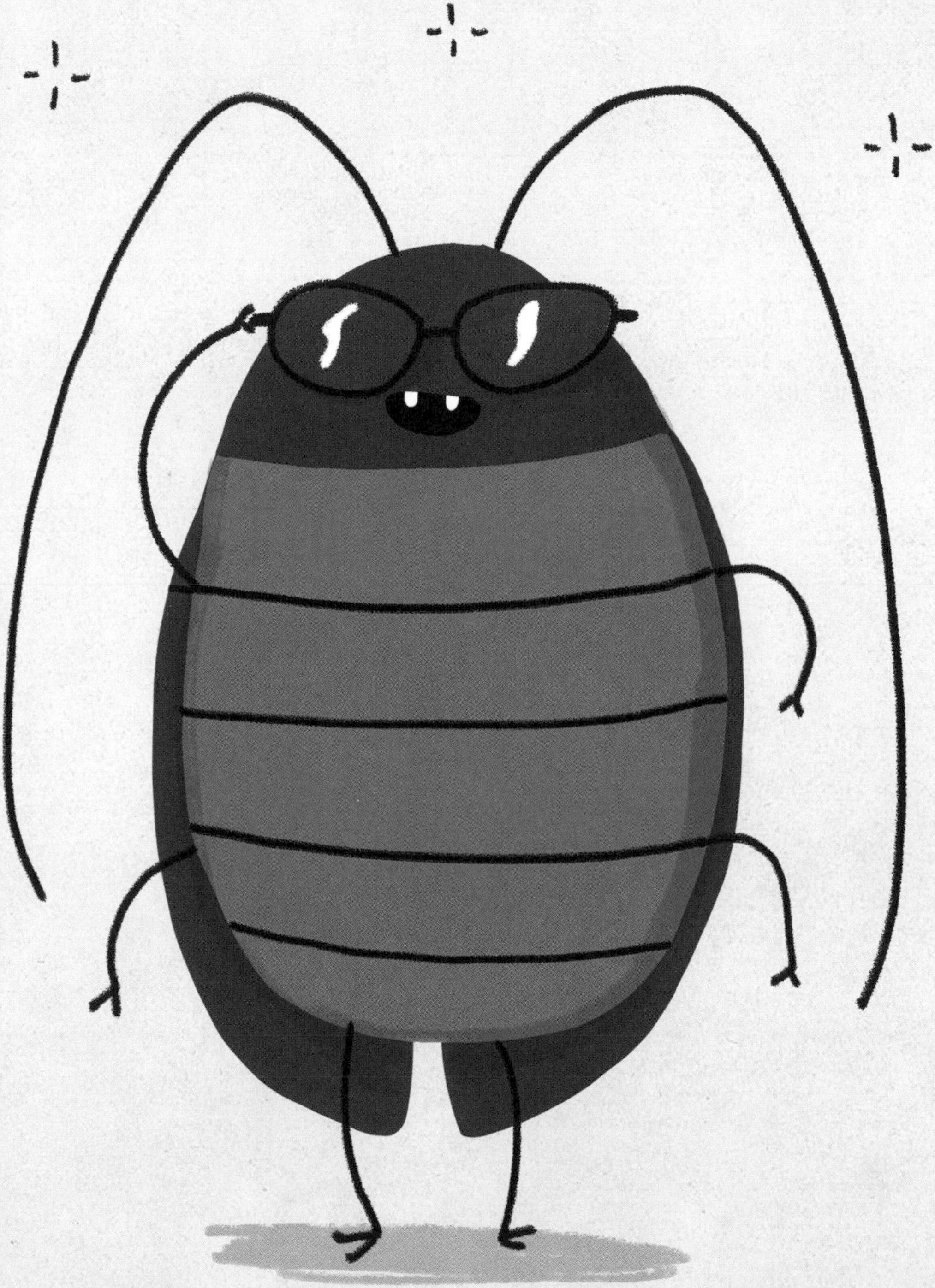

The cockroach likes the heat and dislikes the cold. That's why she seeks

SHELTER

in houses, restaurants and hotels.

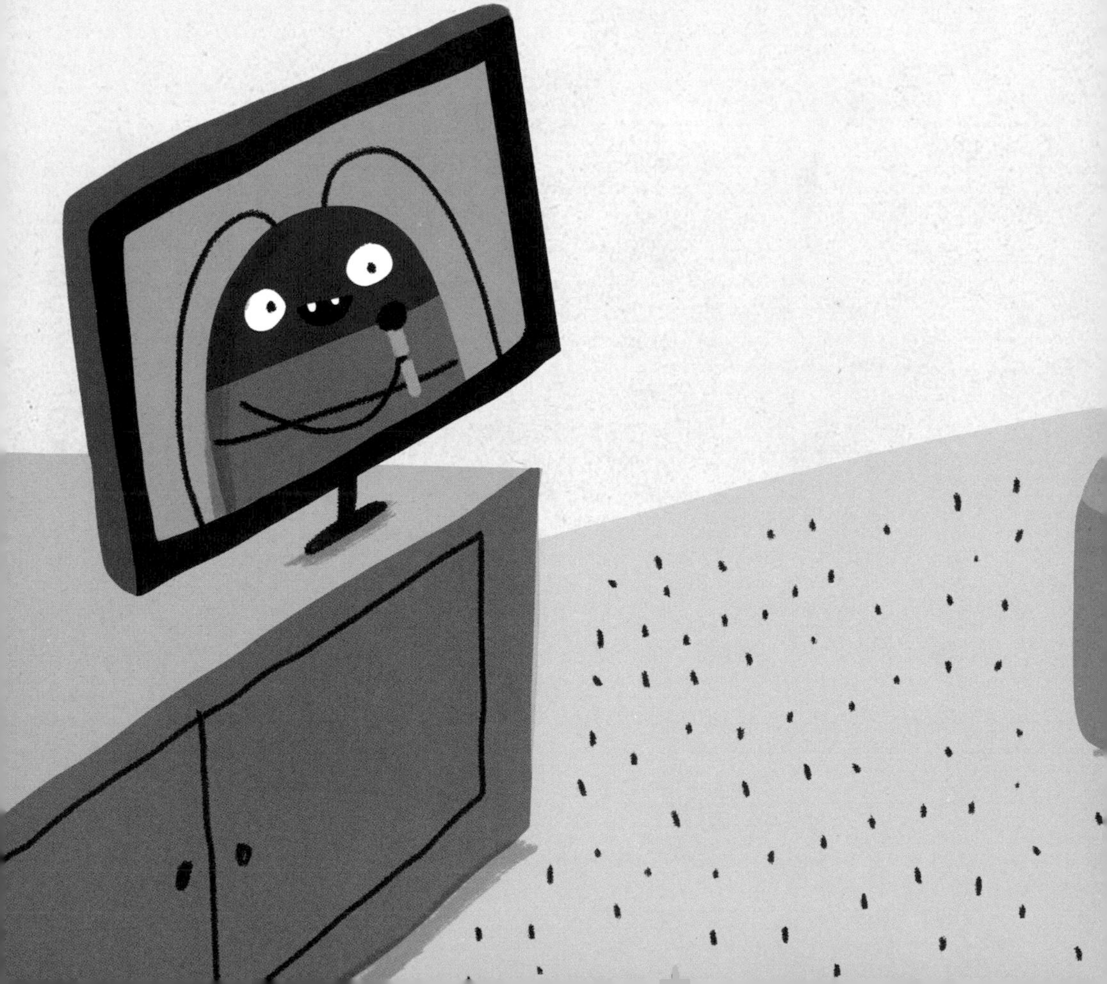

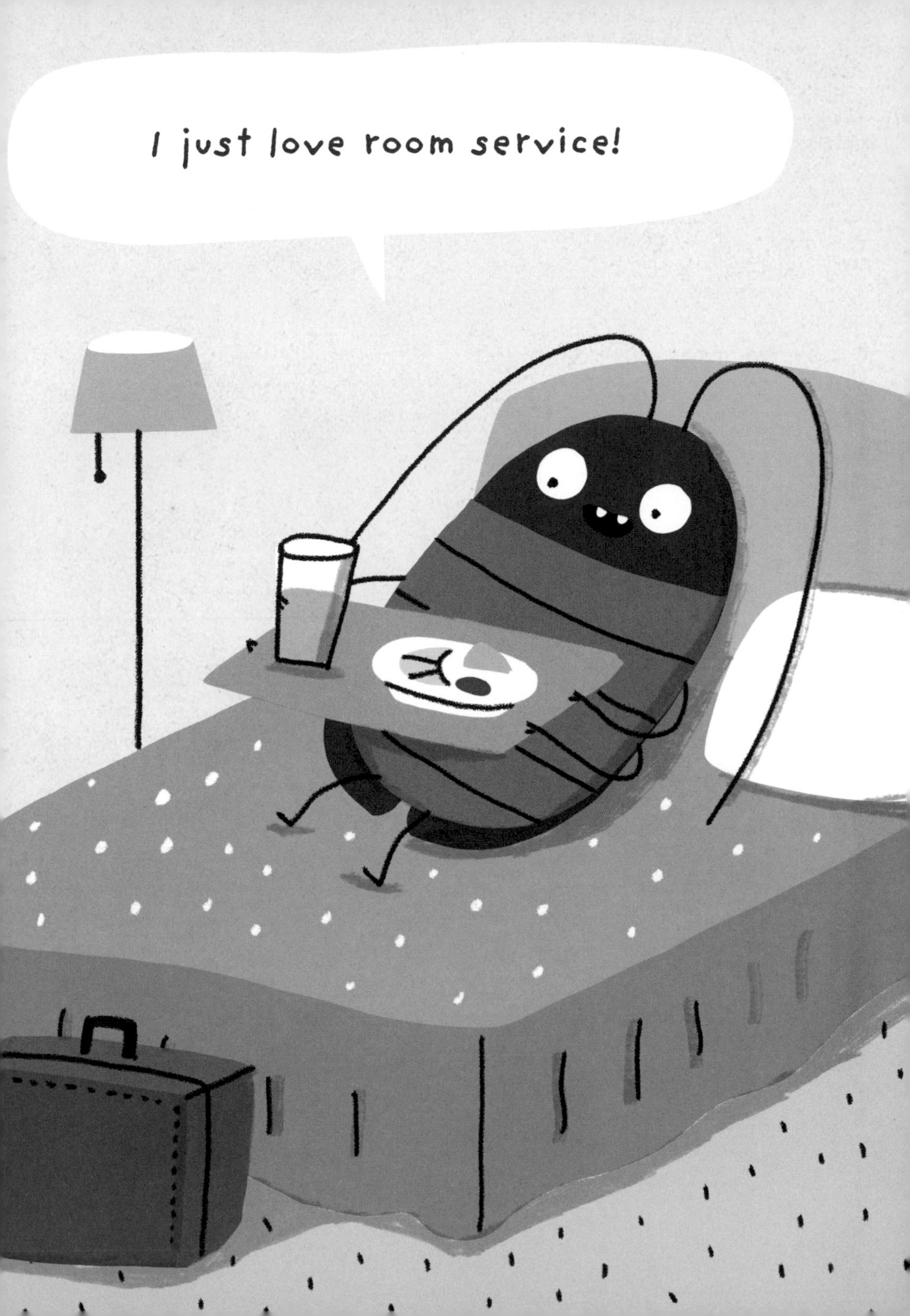
I just love room service!

Like us, the cockroach is an

OMNIVORE:

she eats everything, with a preference for meat and greasy foods. When she's hungry, she will eat just about anything: hair, soap—even nail clippings!

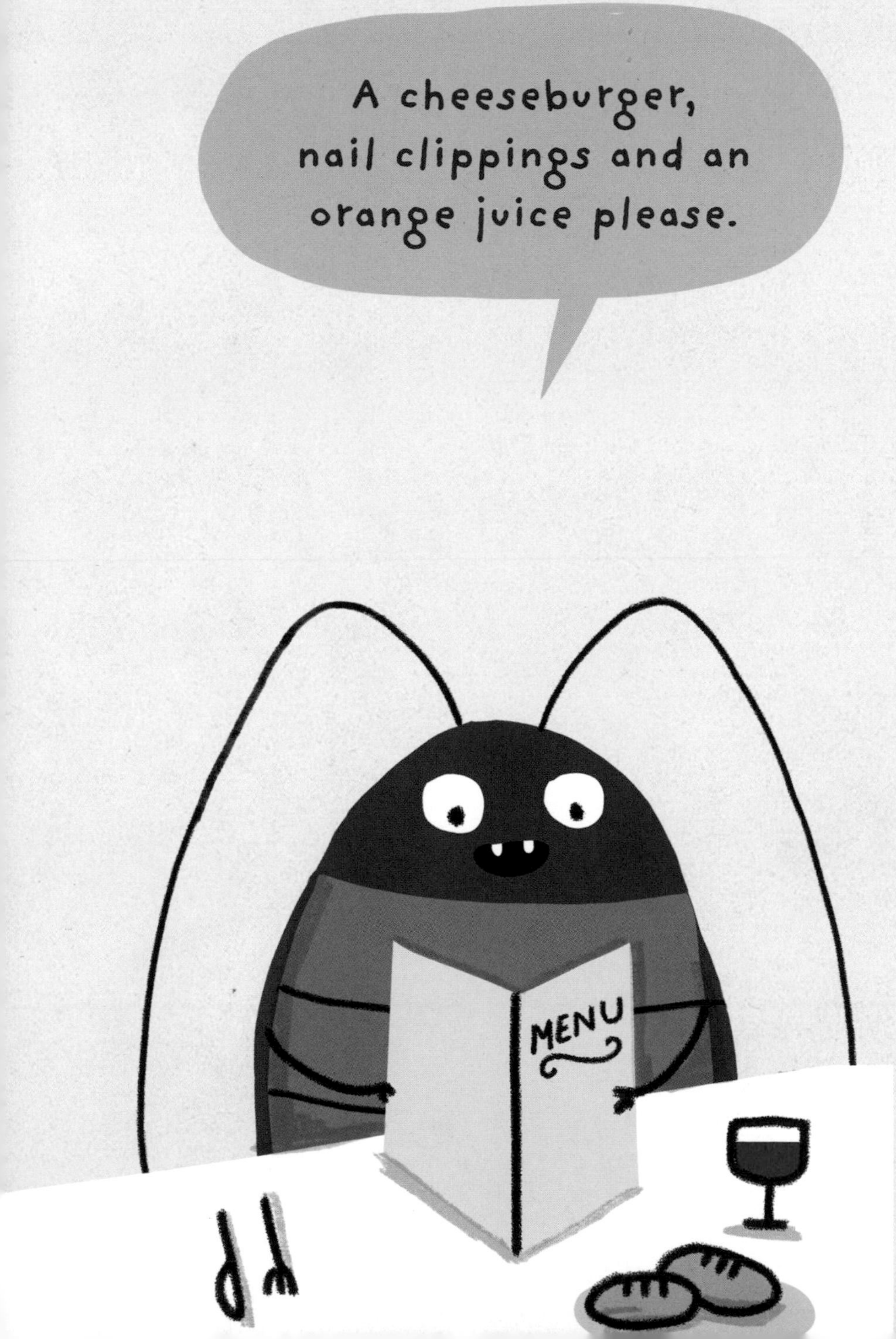
A cheeseburger, nail clippings and an orange juice please.
MENU

The cockroach can come into a house through the plumbing or through the walls. She can also travel from one building to another by hiding in bags and suitcases. When we find her in our houses, it could be because we were unlucky enough to bring this

TRAVELER

home by accident.

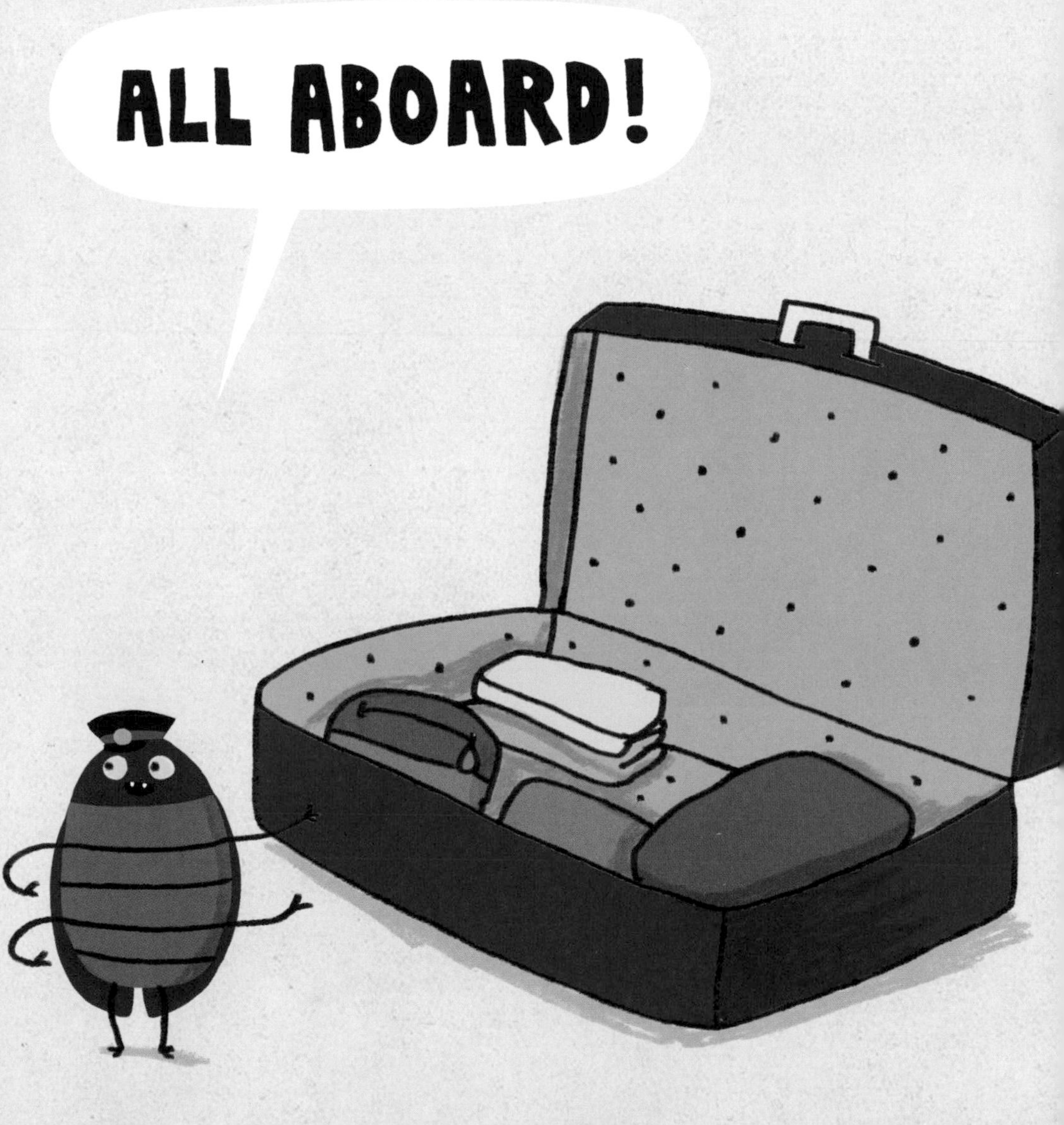
ALL ABOARD!

Humans really don't like sharing their living spaces with the cockroach, and that makes sense because she can carry

GERMS.

She also causes allergies, eats everything in sight and produces bad smells.

PFFFT!

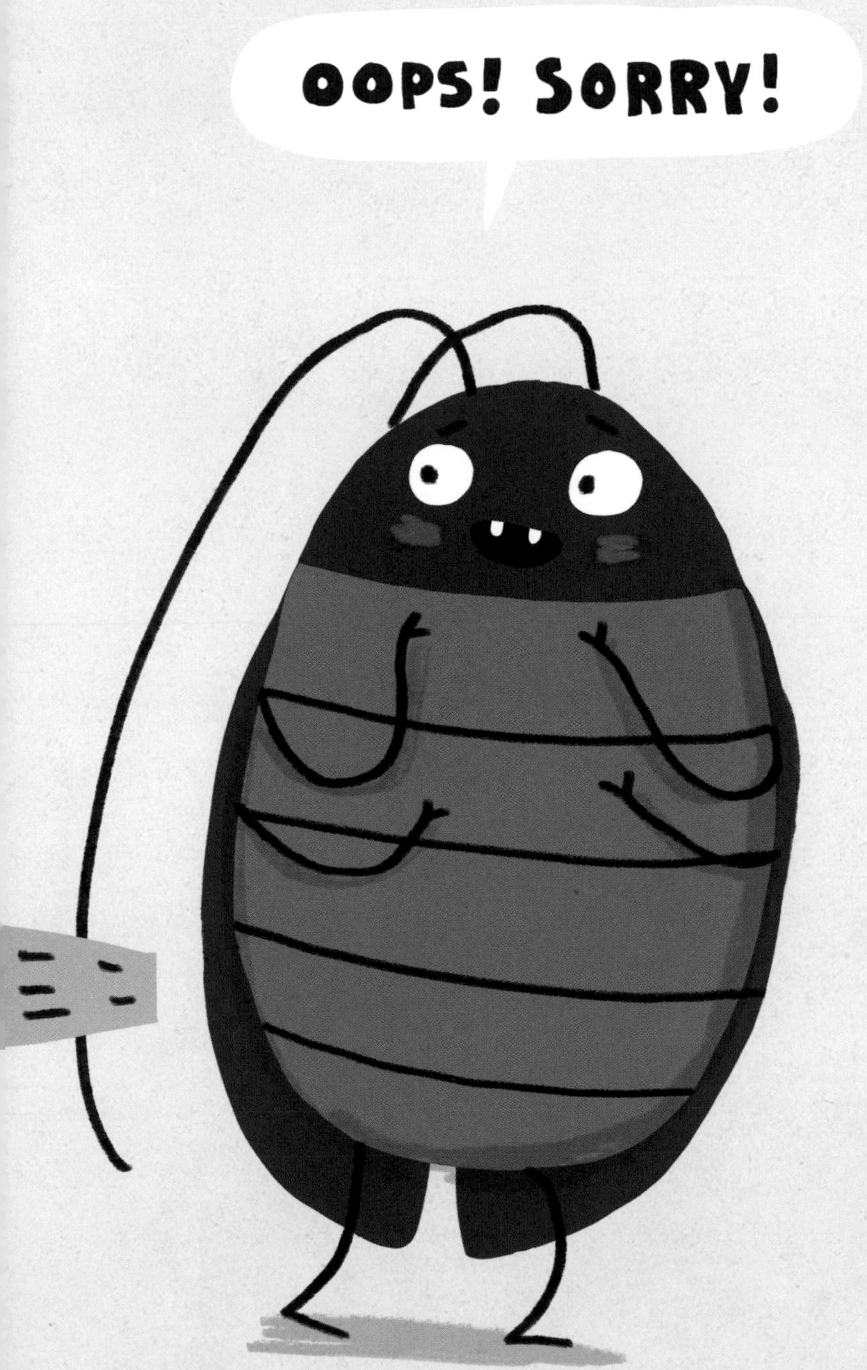
OOPS! SORRY!

On top of everything, the cockroach reproduces very quickly. A female can give birth to hundreds of babies during her lifetime.

Cockroach eggs mature in a case that looks like a purse called an

OOTHECA.

The mother secures the ootheca in a safe space near a food source.

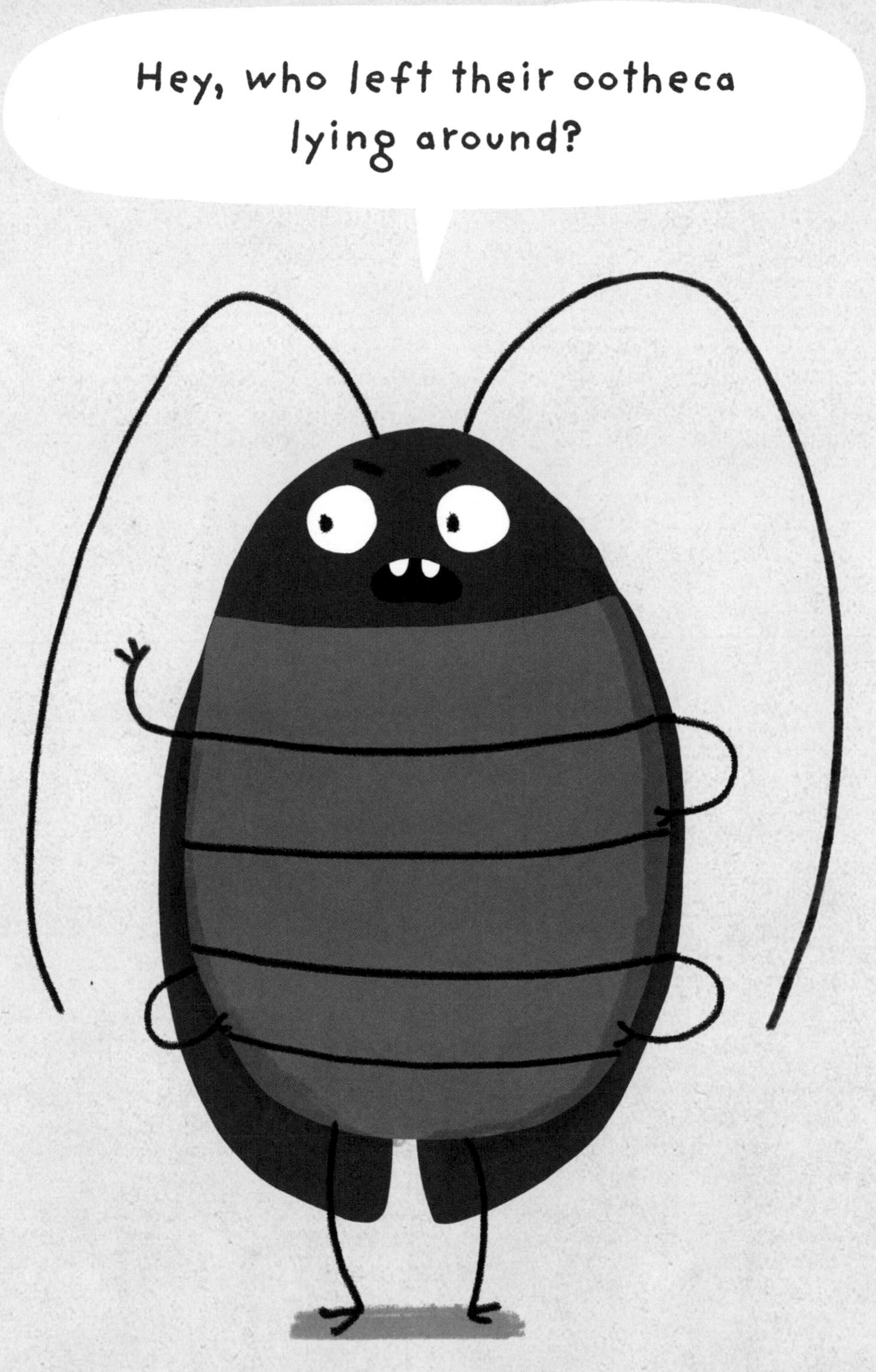
Hey, who left their ootheca lying around?

Up to 16 babies will hatch from the ootheca around

24 HOURS

later. A baby cockroach looks a lot like an adult one but without wings.

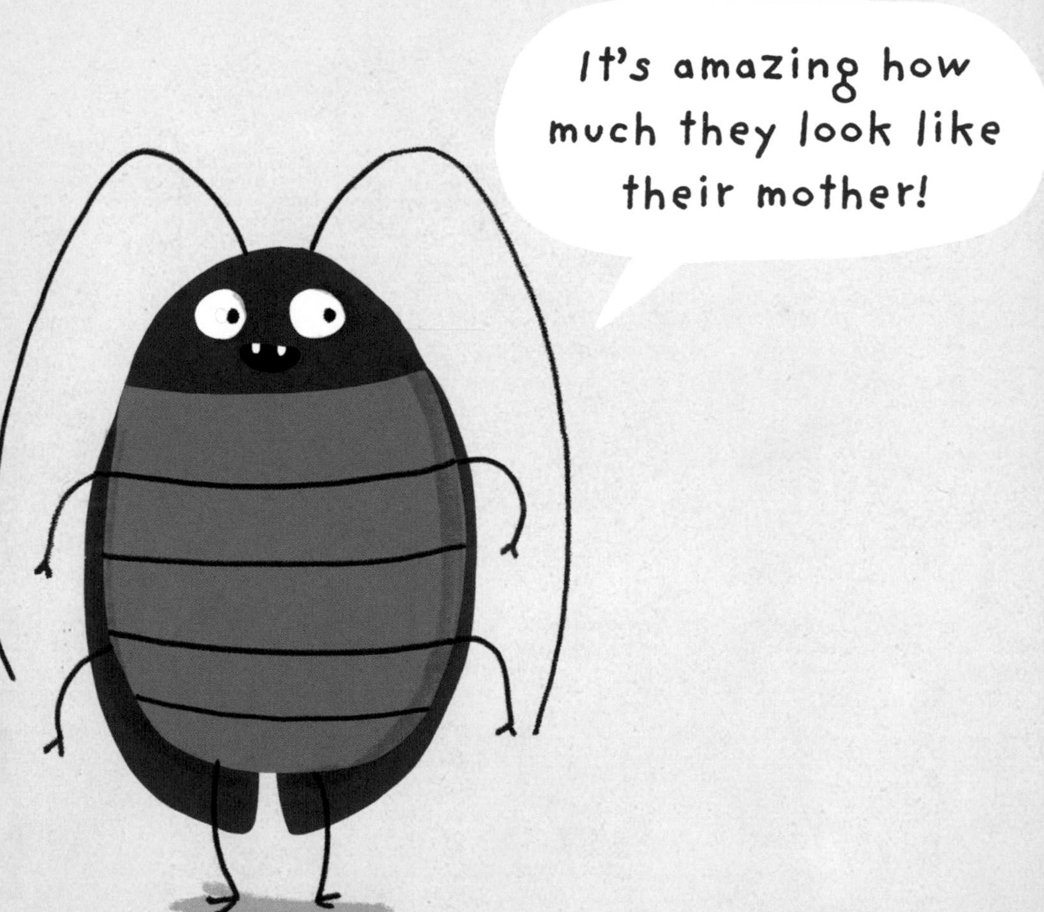
It's amazing how much they look like their mother!

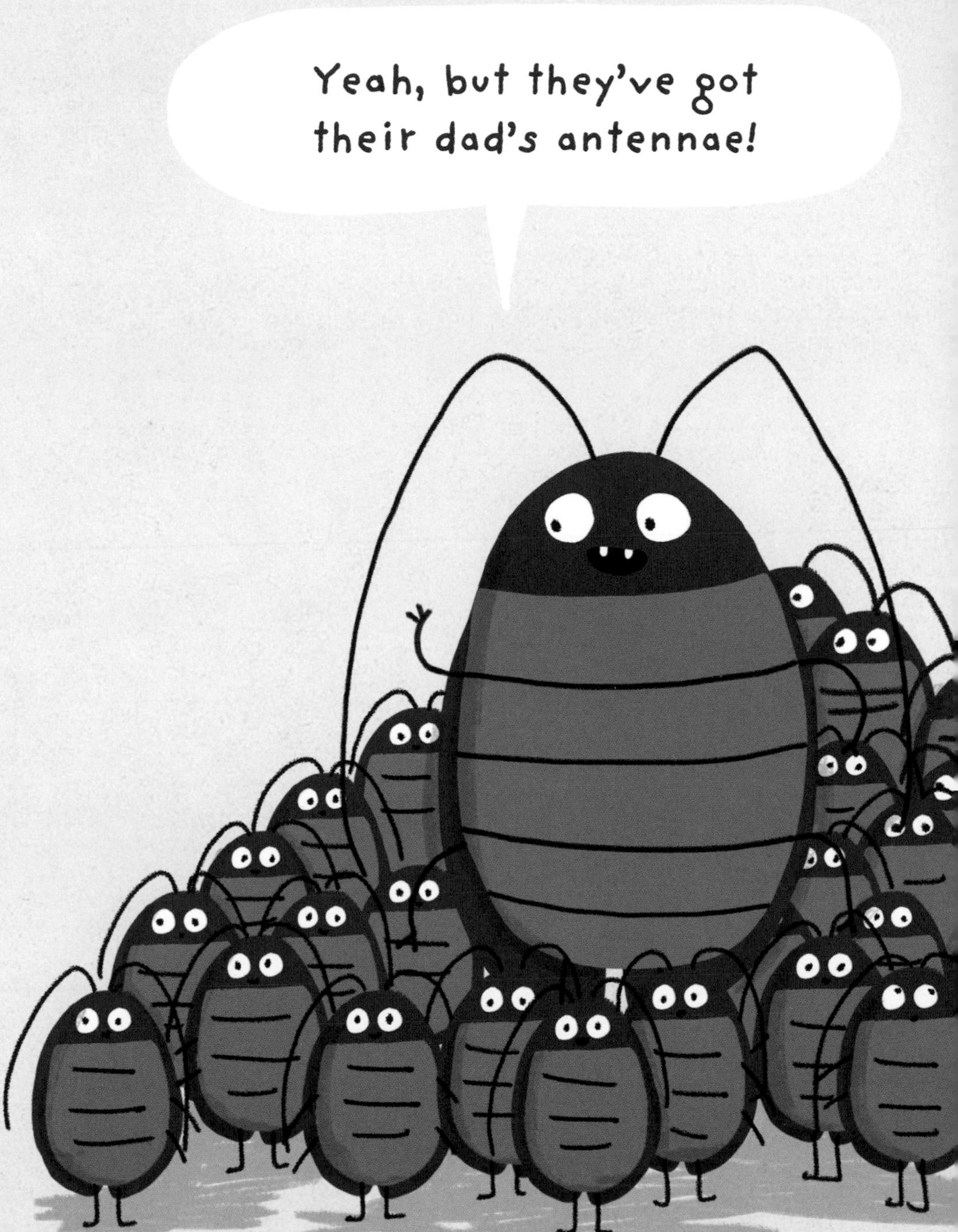
Yeah, but they've got their dad's antennae!

Once the cockroach is well-established in a space, it's really hard to get rid of her. She is very smart and quickly learns to avoid traps set by humans. She can also hide in small spaces like cracks in the floor. Often people have to call an

EXTERMINATOR.

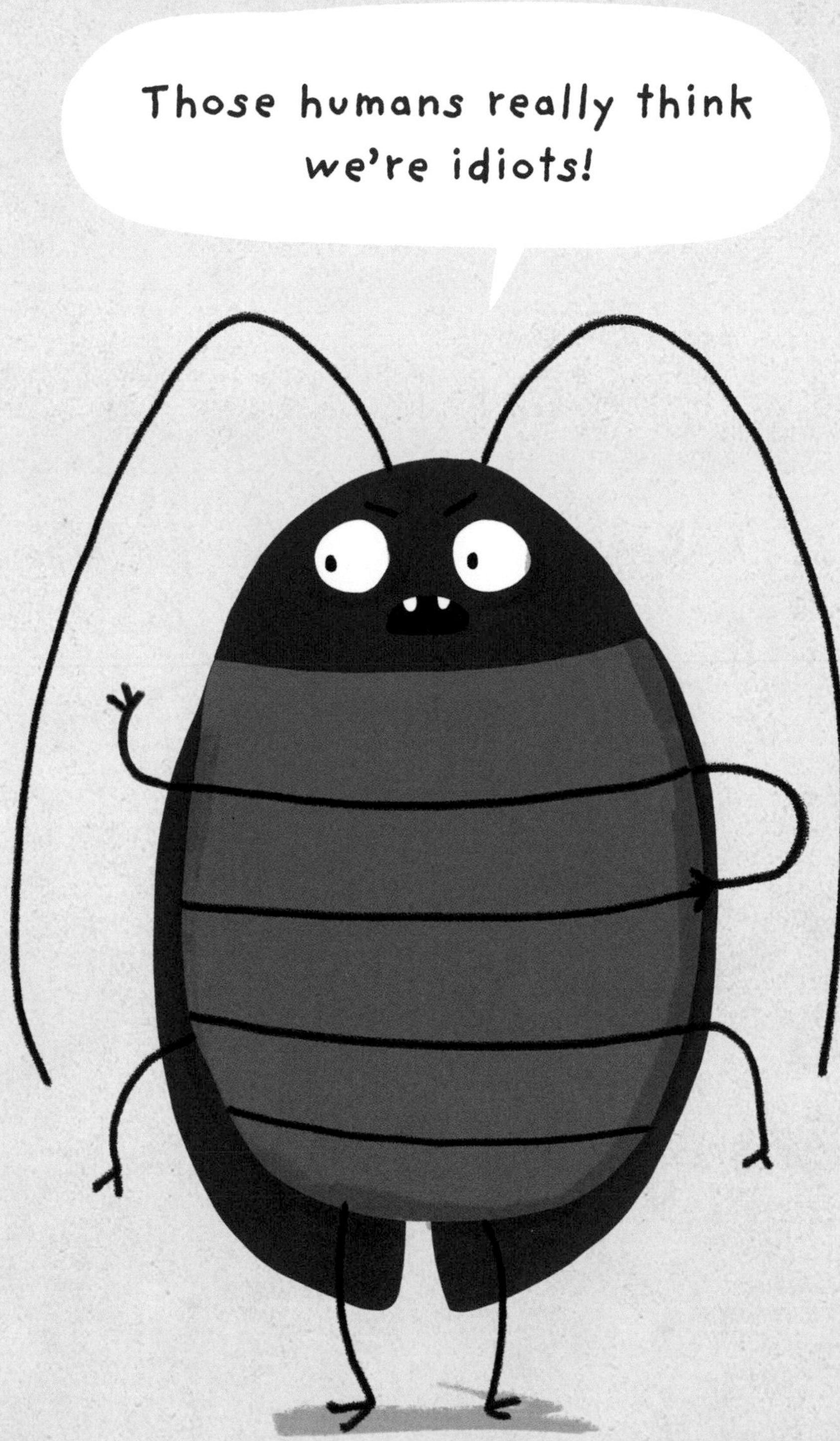
Those humans really think we're idiots!

Cockroaches appeared on Earth over 300 million years ago, and they are not about to disappear anytime soon. So the next time you meet a cockroach,

SHOW RESPECT!

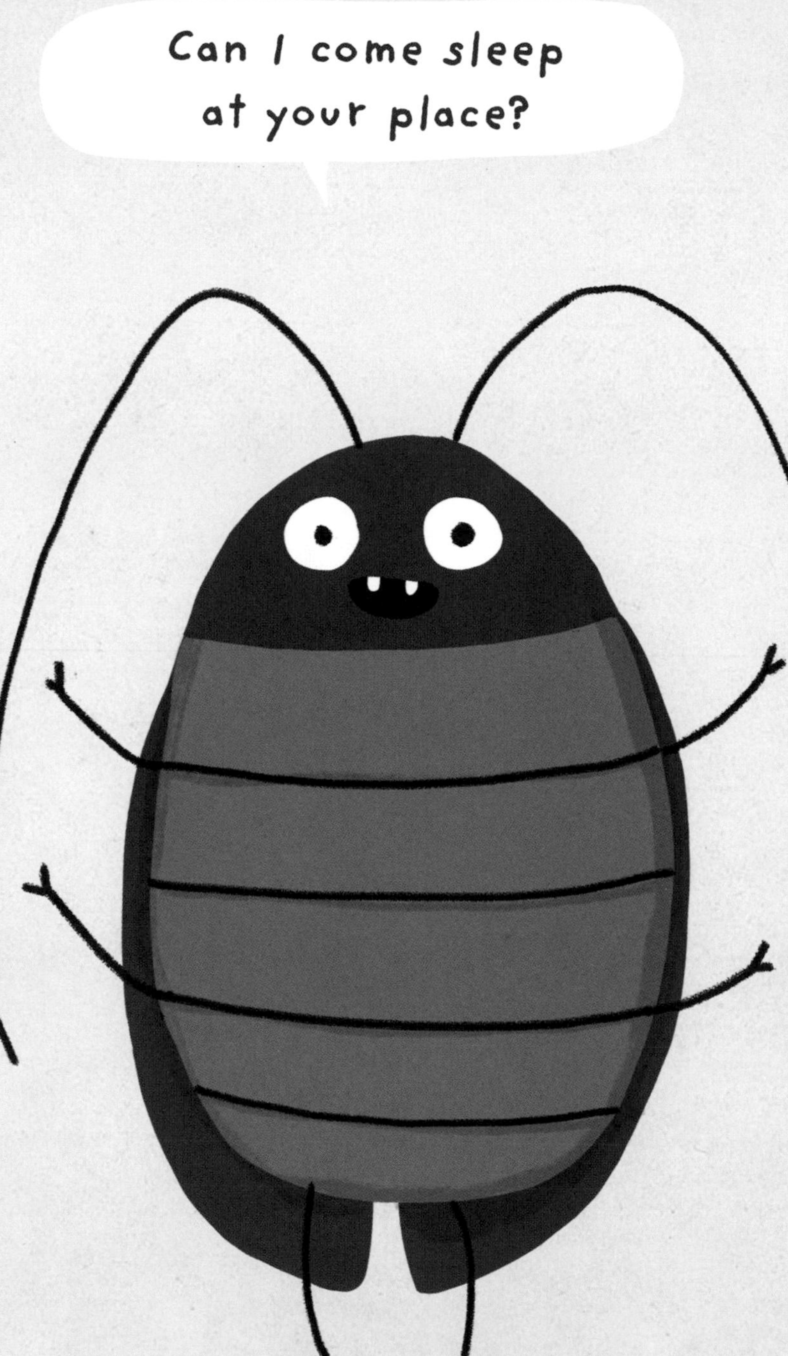
Can I come sleep at your place?

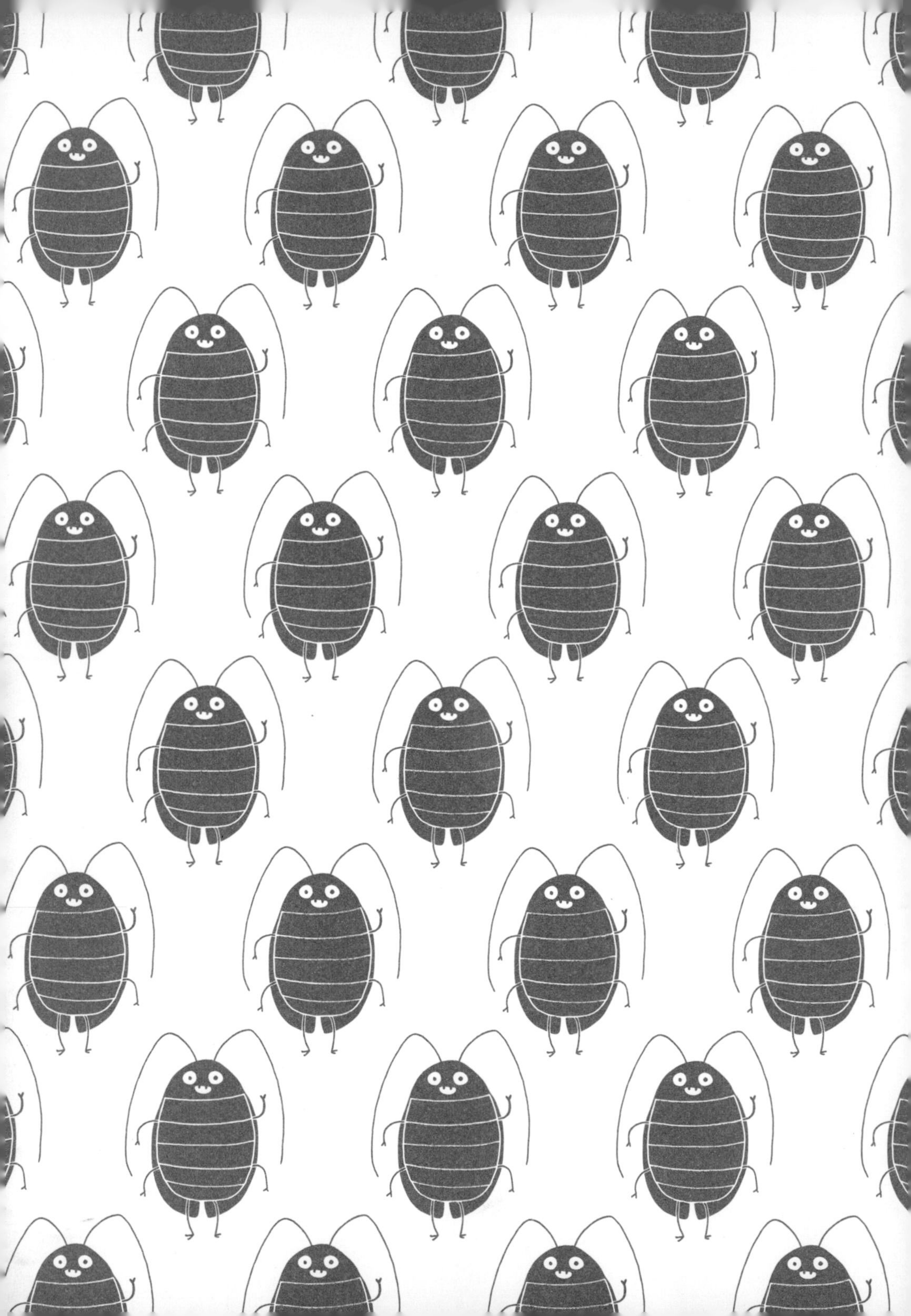